NEW JERSEY

A Scenic Discovery

Printed in Japan.
ISBN 0-89909-049-4

Published by
Foremost Publishers, Inc.
An affiliate of Yankee Publishing Inc.
Dublin, New Hampshire 03444

NEW JERSEY

A Scenic Discovery

Photographed by Walter Choroszewski

Text by John Cunningham

Produced by Foremost Publishers, Inc.

An affiliate of Yankee Publishing Inc.

The rolling waves of summertime call me to the Jersey Shore. Challenging ski slopes in the northwest command my attention in winter. The Piedmont hills are wild with dogwood blooms in springtime, and in the fall brilliantly colored foliage covers a statewide canvas.

This is New Jersey, that 166-mile-long peninsula tucked between the Delaware and Hudson rivers. This is the most densely populated state in the union; avoiding that obvious truth lessens the impact of this remarkable fact that the state is still nearly 75 percent open land.

That open land is what pleases us New Jerseyans. It embraces thick hardwood forests in the north and sprawling pine woodlands in the south. It encompasses rich green marshes behind the familiar sands of the Jersey Shore. It is embodied in vegetable fields to the southwest, where some farms are so huge that giant machines must be used to ensure the harvest of green beans, potatoes, and pickle cucumbers.

I find New Jersey in many ways.

I find it by climbing the tower at High Point atop the Kittatinny Mountains to the northwest.This, as might be expected, is the highest point in the state, 1803 feet above sea level. Atop that monument, as far as my eye can see, a dense hardwood forest spreads away in all directions, broken only by gleaming patches of blue mountain lakes.

I find New Jersey by roaming the 127 miles of the coast, known always as the Jersey Shore. If I seek seaside quiet, that is readily available at the big state-owned park at Island Beach or in little towns such as Surf City, Stone Harbor, or Victorian Cape May. If I seek action, who can overlook Atlantic City's casinos?

And I find New Jersey in the more than one million acres of Pine Barrens in the south. Here is a land largely unspoiled by time, and, indeed, in many areas less settled than it was 125 years ago when the woodland rang with the sounds of now abandoned iron forges and glassworks.

The Pine Barrens are far from a "barrens." That demeaning appelation was bestowed three centuries ago by colonists who could not raise their usual vegetables and fruits in the sandy soil. Botanists have long recognized the Pine Barrens as a precious haven for fauna and flora — including nearly 35 different wild orchids and the richness of cranberries. Some barrens!

New Jersey is much more than open land.

It, is, for one thing, history. The first settlers were here by 1620, at least as early as the Pilgrims of Plymouth. General George Washington spent a total of nearly two years in New Jersey, including three of the first four winters of the American Revolution — twice at Morristown and once at Somerville.

Changing years saw New Jersey in the forefront of history. America's first planned industrial city was founded at Paterson in 1791 to capitalize on the water that thundered down in the Passaic Falls, a 70-foot-high cataract that no longer provides power but still provides magnificent beauty.

People with ideas always have flocked to the state. Thomas Edison arrived in 1870, lived here until his death in 1931. Here he perfected all of his major inventions. Great minds, including Albert Einstein, have come to the more than 600 research laboratories in the state or to the Institute for Advanced Study in Princeton, a place for pure thinking unequalled anywhere.

Geological violence shaped New Jersey hundreds of millions of years ago. Violence cast high the Kittatinny Mountains. It spewed lava across the land to form both the awesome Palisades overlooking the Hudson and the now-peaceful Watchung Mountains. And in that distant past ancient seas laid down the sandy soils that cover the southern two-thirds of the state.

Geologists from around the world look to New Jersey, for here they have found virtually every geological formation. At Franklin, in Sussex County, are found more varieties of minerals than at any place in the world.

Motorists who speed across the state on the New Jersey Turnpike miss the real New Jersey, more's the pity. They see cities and industry (as they usually do wherever superhighways lead) and never even guess at the beauty that is available for those of us who live here.

Somehow New Jersey eludes the words that praise it (and, fortunately, most of the words that damn it). That is because New Jersey is far more than geology or geography, far more than history, far more than industry or agriculture.

It is a flotilla of sailboats on a North Jersey lake, a picnic in one of the state forests. It is the old streets of Cape May, the Gothic splendor of Princeton, the golden dome of the state capitol at Trenton. It is the red and gold that touches North Jersey maple leaves in the fall, the lure of the Jersey Shore in July.

New Jersey is old, New Jersey is new. It struggles to be all things to all people and both succeeds and fails.

See then, tiny, wasp-waisted New Jersey, a land of amazing diversity, a place to brighten the eyes and set the senses afire.

John Cunningham

Cover: The Great Falls, Paterson

11. Day's end in the northwestern Kittatinny Mountains.

12. Water lilies adorn a Pine Barrens pond.

13. Waterloo Village's gristmill merits a splitrail fence.

14. Relaxing time, Victorian style, in a Cape May guest house.

15. When iron boomed, Ringwood Manor knew its glory days.

16. Time out for dock repair at Cold Spring harbor.

17. One sails, the others wait, at Highlands on Sandy Hook Bay.

18. Dawn breaks softly across Somerset County's rolling horse country.

19. Ah, to be in Far Hills when autumn comes again!

20. The Battle of Shoal Harbor flares anew at Port Monmouth.

21. Minuteman in bronze recalls when Springfield held firm in 1780.

22. Shortcake, ice cream, church festivals; it's strawberry time.

23. The big ones never get away on this Tabernacle farm.

24. Revival! Waterfront Hoboken is restoring its solid past.

25. Old Newark, mirrored in the shining faces of a future Newark.

26. Spring snow sugars the Raritan River near High Bridge.

SPRINGFIELD
THE FIRST BRITISH ADVANCE
WAS STAYED AT THE BRIDGE
EAST OF THE VILLAGE JUNE 7 TH
THE BATTLE OF SPRINGFIELD
WAS FOUGHT JUNE 23RD
THE AMERICANS
UNDER GENERAL GREENE
ON THAT DAY NEAR THE BRIDGE
WEST OF THE CHURCH
CHECKED THE ENEMY
WHO IN THEIR RETREAT
BURNED THE CHURCH AND VILLAGE
FROM THIS CHURCH
PARSON CALDWELL TOOK PSALM
DURING THE BATTLE
TO THE AMERICANS
CRYING PUT WATTS
ERECTED BY THE
NEW JERSEY

31. Power plus beauty in the 70-foot-high Passaic Falls at Paterson.

32. Still life in Sussex County's woodland Tillman Ravine.

33. Lake Steenykill, fitting foreground for High Point monument.

34. Ocean Grove: Victorian splendor beside the sea.

35. Baseball and gingerbread architecture mix on a Cape May porch.

36. Fog enshrouds the rugged Delaware Water Gap.

37. Lake Oswego in the Pine Barrens, haunted by morning mist.

38. Blissful are pigs that sleep at the Flemington Fair.

39. The golden grip of summer's setting sun in Neshanic.

40. Winter's icy hand stems the mighty falls at Paterson.

41. The Great Falls, once a mecca for artists, still stirs dreams.

42. Lightning's awesome bolt, unleashed across a Burlington farm.

43. Geese families ignore the rain as they promenade in Wallpack.

44. Ageless, sturdy, artful: a wall in Fairton.

45. Horses, sunset, a towering tree; twilight in Somerset County.

46. Delaware River waters flow placidly through the mighty Gap.

51. Casino land! A rising sun brightens Atlantic City's beach.

52. News and opinion at the general store in Oldwick.

53. Corn meal, coffee, and elixirs: on the shelf at Millbrook.

54. Morning's sun and the spires of Paterson create a fairland.

55. Evening's warm glow settles across the Great Falls.

56. Tenting tonight in the old camp ground at Ocean Grove.

57. Charlie Weaver has rocked on Ocean Grove porches for 50-plus years.

58. No hiking today; snow in Sussex County has closed the Appalachian Trail.

59. Cool, green water in the woods at Hacklebarney State Park.

60. Future cranberry sauce, by the truckload, at Chatsworth.

61. Cranberries turn Chatsworth bogs deep red at harvesttime.

62. Autumn foliage at Peters Valley is rich on nature's canvas.

63. The crops are in; it's time for Lamington farmers to rest.

64. Comforting aloneness: the Deal beach in wintertime.

65. A clam, the shifting sands, and sunshine at Brigantine.

66. Surely, off the Highlands jetty, a bluefish will strike.

60

71. Northwestern New Jersey farms rest beneath icy Sunrise Mountain.

72. Far from the "madding crowd:" Tillman Ravine in Stokes State Forest.

73. April in New Jersey: a colt is momentarily quiet at Port Murray.

74. Bird's eye view of the northwestern dairyland.

75. Lake Wawayanda, crystal clear in a North Jersey state park.

76. Inside, the State Capitol is three stories of balconied elegance.

77. The golden dome at Trenton, symbol of state government.

78. Black River & Western RR conductors in Flemington are patient waiters.

79. All aboard! Commuter trains at Bernardsville wait for no one.

80. Wish you were here; postcard time at the Congress Hall in Cape May.

81. This is Seaside Heights; it could be almost anywhere on the Jersey Shore.

82. Last resting place: the Millstone Presbyterian Church cemetery.

83. Angel detail on an 18th century tombstone in Springfield.

84. Can winter be far behind? Autumn leaves on the Flatbrookville road.

85. Tradition in the saddle: fox hunts are usual fare in Somerset County.

86. Old Barnegat lighthouse, lordly amid Long Beach Island's dunes.

91. Winter has fastened its cold hand on a Mt. Salem farm.

92. What tangled webs a spider weaves, as proved in the Ramapo Mountains.

93. Private enterprise thrives at Three Bridges: 10 cents a glass.

94. Everyone digs for bait along the Sandy Hook strand.

95. Great Bay at Tuckerton, a fisherman's way of life.

96. The old red mill at Clinton, being captured on canvas.

97. Painting in Imlaystown does not require art lessons.

98. Nature has reclaimed this yard inside a Millbrook Village fence.

99. Buttermilk Falls, deep in the forests on Kittatinny Mountain slopes.

100. Horses are New Jersey's fastest growing farm commodity.

101. Old and valuable: antiques in a Mullica Hill shop.

102. Blair Hall at Princeton University is the best of Gothic.

103. Princeton memorial to soldiers who fought there in 1777.

104. Nothing seems to change the tranquil town of Delaware.

105. Fairs dominate summer dreams in all New Jersey farm areas.

106. Wind tides on the Jersey Shore.

111. The fleet's in at the fishing pier at Point Pleasant.

112. George Washington Bridge, high above the Hudson River.

113. Phragmites (or "foxtails") are eloquent at Port Norris.

114. Once the Clinton dam powered mills; now trout lurk in its flow.

115. Backlight does wonders for a thistle plant near Somerville.

116. Tides, storms, winds: nothing deters Sandy Hook's anglers.

117. Point Pleasant lobstermen wouldn't trade places with anyone.

118. The pond at Fairton is small; sunset makes it magnificient.